THE AROOSTOOK ARMS RACE

COLD WAR IN THE CROWN OF MAINE

AREND T. THIBODEAU

AMERICA
THROUGH
TIME

This book is dedicated to the men and women of the United States Armed Forces and the hardworking residents of Aroostook County

Special thanks to Charlie Cormier, Cuppy Johndro of The Loring Museum, and John C. Garbinski.

I also wish to acknowledge the support and generosity extended to me by property owners Matt Field, Sue St. Pierre, and the Mi'kmaq Nation.

America Through Time®
An imprint of SUTTON PUBLISHING INC
www.through-time.com

First published 2025

ISBN 978-1-63499-512-2

Typeset in 10pt on 13pt Sabon
Printed and bound in the United States of America

PREFACE

As a lifelong resident of Maine, it was only recently when I visited Caribou in "The County" and I became enchanted with this area of northern Maine upon my very first visit. The people in the northlands are welcoming and friendly with a strong work ethic and integrity that is unequalled in other regions of the state.

Aroostook County (also known as "The County") is Maine's largest, northernmost county, which according to the 2021 census has a population of around 67,000. The County is rich in resources, with 2,000 bodies of water and a total land area which constitutes 21.2 percent of Maine's lands.

Even though it is far removed from Maine's idyllic rocky coast, Aroostook County is a prime example of quintessential Maine where residents tolerate harsh winters, remote locations, and unforgiving wilderness. Mainers from the County are a tough breed that endure many hardships to carve out a way of life.

Despite the remoteness of the area and the unforgiving conditions, the County is enchanting. There is something about life in Northern Maine that is reminiscent of a time when humans had to tame the lands to make a living, braving tremendous difficulties to prosper and persevere.

Enchantments aside, as I explored this region of Maine, I began to uncover a dark past in Aroostook County. As residents went about their lives working in the potato fields, harvesting timber in the woodlands, and going about their routines, the United States was amassing a weapons stockpile that would rival even the most vivid imagination as they prepared for nuclear war. Weapons of mass destruction were poised, ready to go at a moment's notice and often hidden right under the collective nose of society.

The resilience of its residents and its geographical location made this region of Maine a logical choice to build a strategic air defense center when World War II concluded and the need for American air superiority became paramount in the defense of our nation.

The secret stockpile really began to intrigue me, and the more I discovered, the more I came to realize just how important Aroostook County was to United States military strategy and the security of our nation.

Some of the infrastructure and development in this area was quite well known and difficult to hide, but even more was buried in secrecy. Top secret areas cordoned off with multiple layers of security fencing, armed guards with dogs walking the perimeter, all concealing a massive nuclear weapons stockpile that remained classified until the late 1990s.

Please join me as I investigate this extremely volatile and active time in our nation's history, discussing the Cold War era, uncovering what has been left behind, and exploring the future of Aroostook County.

CONTENTS

INTRODUCTION

In the seventeenth century, early English settlers encountered majestic white pines that grew to towering heights along the coast of present-day Maine and proclaimed them to be perfect for masts in shipbuilding; since that time, the Pine Tree State has been known for its abundance of resources.

However, it was not the resources alone that gave Maine a strategic advantage. Its geographical location makes it the first line of defense in the North Atlantic, and that became especially important at the end of World War II when the European landscape changed significantly.

Life in Aroostook County during the post-World War II period was typical of small-town America where farmlands were dominant. Vast farms dominated hundreds of acres and thousands more were occupied by working forests. The area was largely unpopulated, and during the period preceding World War II, large plots of undeveloped land were visible as far as the eye could see. Potato and timber harvesting were the primary occupations, and life was simple and laidback. Community support was strong, everyone knew their neighbor, and families had ancestral farms that supported them for generations.

As the entire nation celebrated the end of World War II, the mood in the County was jubilant as well. America and her freedoms remained intact; evil had been defeated. Tyranny and oppression had been fought against and the oppressors lost.

However, just as the end of World War II signaled the closing of army air force fields in Houlton and Presque Isle (both in Aroostook County), a new threat was emerging, and a new era was about to begin.

The Soviet Union (who once allied with Great Britan and the United States to defeat Germany) created tensions at the end of the war as the communist nation's territories grew and they became a significant power in eastern Europe.

Emerging from World War II as the superpower of the Eastern Bloc, Soviet ideologies quickly clashed with those of the western superpowers and a new age of warfare began.

1
THE COLD WAR

Most of us are aware of the Cold War and the ideological clash that occurred as both the United States and Soviet Union flexed their proverbial muscles. The former was a democratic and influencing member of the Western Allies, and the latter, the controlling power of the Eastern Bloc, led by Joseph Stalin in communist Russia. For more than four decades, each country amassed massive nuclear arms stockpiles which began at the end of World War II when the two countries emerged from the war as reigning superpowers.

The United States had harnessed atomic energy, and the world watched as it demonstrated its power in Japan. On September 2, 1945, the United States had emerged victoriously from World War II, firmly established as a world superpower with fission capabilities. However, United States' atomic capabilities were a short-lived deterrent, and as the Soviet Union continued to grow and develop its own fission technology, the United States saw the need to reaffirm its position on the global field, so in July 1947 the National Defense Act was passed. Shortly thereafter, the Department of the Air Force was established on September 18, 1947.

It is also worth noting that in 1945, English writer George Orwell penned the term "Cold War" in an article published in *The Tribune* on October 19.[1] Little did he know that the country was about to embark on a decades-long war with no shots fired. The term Cold War became popular following the publication of this article and is still used today to describe this tense period in human history.

Since there was no official declaration of war and the Cold War did not result in any direct conventional warfare between the United States and Russia, there is no official beginning to it. However, on March 5, 1946, Winston Churchill accompanied President Harry S. Truman to Westminster College in Fulton, Missouri, where he gave a speech outlining the concern for a potential Soviet buildup in Europe. In the speech he titled "The Sinews of Peace," Churchill spoke these famous words: "From Stettin in the Baltic to Trieste in the Adriatic, an iron curtain has descended across the continent."[2]

The opening and closing dates of the Cold War are ambiguous, but Churchill's speech established the term Iron Curtain and ushered in the unofficial start of the Cold War.

The U.S. then began an arms race with the Soviet Union, amassing a defense infrastructure and weapons stockpile that would create military budgeting strains and worldwide anxiety for decades. Weapons of mass destruction were poised, ready to go at a moment's notice and often hidden right in plain sight within built-up areas and rural locations alike. Secret weapons storage facilities and stockpiles were created unbeknownst to the communities that hosted them, and society at large went about their lives oblivious to the magnitude of weapons being stored in their backyards. The age of economic tensions, propaganda, covert intelligence, and arms buildup had begun. It was the age of the Cold War.

The unlikely allies of World War II. Winston Churchill, Harry S. Truman, and Josef Stalin. Stalin's territorial advancements created tensions at the end of the war which would lead to the Cold War.[3]

Right: The mushroom cloud produced by the bomb at Nagasaki, Japan, on September 1, 1945. The development of the atomic bomb in both the U.S. and the Soviet Union would hasten the pace of the Cold War.[4]

Below: Churchill and Truman on the presidential train arriving in Fulton, Missouri, where Churchill would deliver his "Sinews of Peace" speech.[5]

2
AROOSTOOK COUNTY

Airborne warfare developed in World War I and became increasingly important as conventional warfare progressed and aircraft evolved. By the end of World War II, the war effort had become dependent on airborne warfare. The United States' defeat of Japan would not have been possible without the use of *Enola Gay*, a B-29 Superfortress which dropped atomic bombs on both Hiroshima and Nagasaki, Japan, effectively ending the war.

However, it was not the air force that made these fateful bombing runs. Before the signing of the National Defense Act and the corresponding creation of the air force, U.S. air superiority was established by the United States Army Air Forces (USAAF).

It was the USAAF which first introduced residents of Aroostook County to military aircraft and infrastructure. Houlton Army Airfield was activated in 1941 and was closed in 1944. When the airfield closed, all personnel were transferred to the Presque Isle Army Airfield.

The Presque Isle Army Airfield was constructed as a commercial airport in 1930. The U.S. government activated it as an army airfield on September 15, 1941, and it was operated by Army Transport Command and the 23rd Army Air Force Ferrying Wing. The base closed when World War II ended. However, that was not the end of the Presque Isle airfield, and we will return to it later.

The newly formed U.S. Air Force established the Strategic Air Command (SAC) that began to consider locations for SAC bases, and special consideration was given to new navigational methods that enabled aircraft to traverse the Artic Circle, reaching targets of primary concern in the Soviet Union. The shortest routes to these locations in the Soviet Union originated from the Northeastern United States. It was decided that Limestone, Maine, in Aroostook County was to be the location of a new strategic bomber base. The New England Division of the Army Corps of Engineers selected a location in the northeastern part of Limestone Township that extended into Caswell Plantation.

In the northeast corner of Aroostook County, Limestone township is 10 miles from Caribou as the crow flies. The quiet little north Maine town had a population of 1,855 residents in 1940, and within the next decade, it was about to experience both a dramatic influx of residents and a robust infrastructure buildup.

Aroostook is the second largest county east of the Mississippi. Strategically, its location made it the closest U.S. County to targets that were in the Soviet Union. An abundance of limestone and other raw materials allowed construction crews to quarry their own materials, saving the cost of transporting raw materials into the area.

Above: A 1940 landscape photo depicting potato fields along the Aroostook River, taken just outside of Caribou, near Limestone, Maine.[1]

Below: The town of Limestone was connected to the rail system in Maine by the Bangor and Aroostook Railroad in 1895. By the beginning of the twentieth century, most all points in Maine were connected by railroad.[2]

3

LIMESTONE AIR FORCE BASE (LORING)

On April 5, 1947, the U.S. Army Corps of Engineers (USACE) was given authorization to begin construction on Limestone airfield. At the time, *Engineering News Record* reported that the project was representative of "much of the thinking of the men who must fly, service and support the products of the aircraft designers' art."[1] From its inception, the base was an innovative first of its kind.

On May 23, 1947, a $17 million contract was awarded for phase one construction of the Limestone airbase consisting of a north–south runway, parallel taxiway with parking apron, a base operations building with a control tower, an electric power plant, water supply system, railroad spur, a 250-man barracks, and an arch hangar.

The site was ideal for the construction of a strategic base. The slightly elevated location provided distance from the prime farmland where potato farms flourished, and aside from the timber, the wetlands and uncultivated areas offered little commercial or agricultural value. The area was relatively free of obstacles, at an elevation that prevented the formation of ground fog, and building materials were abundantly available. Hard bedrock was used as a base for facility foundations as well as the runway; the airfield was to be the first of its kind in the world. The USACE wasted no time awarding contracts to build an impressive infrastructure in the defense of the United States and its positions abroad. It was designed specifically to meet the requirements as a SAC base, incorporating considerations for strategy and heavy aircraft which would be operating at high speeds.

Aside from atomic weapons, the newly developed B-36 "Peacemaker" bomber was a key component in the early days of the Cold War, as well as in the planning and development of Limestone airfield. The United States anticipated the arrival of the aircraft to their bomber inventory in 1948–1949. With a range of 12,000 miles, it was the first aircraft to be considered "intercontinental" by SAC.

As technology progressed in the atomic world, so too did the need to transport the large and cumbersome weapons, and the B-36 could carry any of the nuclear weapons in the U.S. arsenal within its bay without any modifications to the compartment. In addition to whatever payload the B-36 needed to carry, the bomber weighed 300,000 pounds, so even more considerations had to be made when designing the infrastructure for these heavy aircraft. Limestone was selected as the first base location in the United States to be designed specifically for the B-36, and the arch hangar created to accommodate the large bombers was a marvel of modern engineering in its design and construction.

The arch hangar was large enough to accommodate two B-36 aircraft and was one of two arch hangars simultaneously built in the U.S. At the time it was built, the B-36 arch hangar was the largest in the world. Designed by Anton Tedesko for Roberts & Shaefer of Chicago, this first-generation B-36 arch hangar is a monolith that measures 370 feet by 314 feet and provides 106,760 square feet of unobstructed floor space. Thin-shelled, reinforced concrete used in the construction of the arch was considered cutting-edge engineering technology at the time of its design and construction.

Special considerations for the harsh Maine winters and deep frosts had to be factored in when designing and building the runway. More than 2 million cubic yards of earth were removed, and flexible bituminous-concrete pavement was used in building the impressive airstrip that would accommodate the B-36 "Peacemaker" bomber.[2]

The base was slowly evolving, but winter and funding was slowing the progress of building, and by 1950, the base only had nineteen officers and 172 airmen stationed there. Then, on June 25, 1950, communist North Korea crossed the 38th parallel, invading South Korea. SAC had its first opportunity for combat and soon demonstrated its full capabilities and expanded quickly. In 1951, increased military funding accelerated construction at Limestone; the runway was also extended at this time, in addition to eight new hangars being built.

By the latter part of 1952, the base had grown exponentially, and in February 1953, SAC commander General Curtis E. LeMay visited. While he was inspecting the base for readiness, he indicated that Limestone was ready for full operations with an assigned bombardment wing. On February 15, 1953, base command was transferred from USAAC to SAC. The 42nd Bombardment Wing was activated, and on February 25, 1953, Limestone Air Force Base became operational.

During this period, a great deal of emphasis was placed on training and operational readiness. Ten B-36 aircraft arrived in April 1953, and by the end of August, the wing had twenty-seven bombers.

On October 1, 1953, Limestone Air Force Base was renamed Loring Air Force Base in honor of fallen Medal of Honor recipient and Maine native Charles Joseph Loring, who lost his life in action during the Korean War when he heroically flew his disabled F-80 Shooting Star into an enemy artillery position and destroyed it.

The 42nd Bombardment Wing was declared operationally capable of implementing its emergency war plan on January 7, 1954. The year 1954 saw more build-up as Loring AFB was declared a staging area for fighter-aircraft *en route* between the United States and Europe. With the additional transient traffic, and Loring's sixty-three assigned aircraft, Loring had become a fully operational air force base, and a highly valuable asset to SAC.

Construction continued at Loring AFB and the arch hangar was soon dwarfed by the heavy bomber double-cantilever hangar which was built in 1955. The DC hangar was built in response to SAC's need for larger, more efficient maintenance hangars, and this second generation of maintenance hangar was another of the many engineering feats accomplished during the buildup at Loring AFB. This impressive three-bay hangar is roughly 250 feet by 600 feet, and the hangar was paramount to the bomber maintenance program at Loring. It was capable of housing five B-36s or six B-52s and was the first and only hangar with these capabilities. The heavy bomber DC hangar contributed greatly to SAC's mission of maintaining a fleet at optimal peak readiness; the impressive stature of the DC hangar is one of the dominating features of Loring's abandoned skyline to this day.

The arms buildup persisted as the Cold War continued and Loring grew. As Russia developed fusion technology and the Soviet nuclear program grew, so too did SAC's mission of peacekeeping through containment. By the mid-1950s, Loring housed four bombardment squadrons, refueling and maintenance squadrons, a tactical hospital, an air force hospital, an air police squadron, and numerous other squadrons in support of SAC's peacekeeping mission.

As the Cold War evolved, so did its weapons and weapons delivery systems. The Boeing B-52 Stratofortress was an all-jet heavy bomber that replaced the B-36 in the mid-1950s. June 16, 1956, marked the arrival of the first permanent B-52 to Loring AFB, and the 42nd BW at Loring AFB was the first B-36 unit to transition to the new B-52 Stratofortress. As a symbol of the aircraft's versatility and intercontinental abilities, it was christened with both Atlantic and Pacific Ocean waters and aptly given the name *State of Maine*. By February 1957, the 42nd BW achieved combat-ready status with a full complement of B-52s. The last B-36 left Loring AFB on September 6, 1956.[3]

By 1957, advances in refueling technologies were able to match advances being made to bomber technology, and the first KC-135 Stratotanker arrived at Loring on October 16, 1957. The KC-135 served as a replacement for the KC-97, and the first to arrive at Loring was christened *Aroostook Queen*. It could match the altitude and speed of the B-52, and by April 1958, twenty KC-135 Stratotankers had arrived in Loring. The 42nd Air Refueling Squadron attained combat-ready status in May.

Aside from the direct aircraft support, Loring had other impressive infrastructure features such as a 189-mile-long pipeline that stretched from Limestone to the coastal town of Searsport. There, sea-going tankers would bring fuel into the deepwater port where it would be sent to Loring via a 6-inch-diameter pipeline.

Although it all came under Loring's control in the 1960s, North River Depot began to appear on the northeastern side of Limestone, right around the time Loring's construction was nearing completion.

The B-36 "Peacekeeper" bomber sits on a tarmac beside its much smaller predecessor, the B-29. U.S. Army Air Forces, Washington, D.C., *c.* 1942.[4]

With scaffolding, cranes, and lots of steel standing by, construction of the arch hangar was underway at Limestone Airfield in 1948.[5]

Crews working on the roof of the arch hangar getting the scaffolding and framework into place in preparation of pouring the concrete.[6]

A B-36 Peacemaker bomber sits under an arch that is under construction with an aircraft tug parked in front of it.[7]

Workers laying bituminous concrete on the runway and taxiway areas, 1948. Engineers negated the deep frosts encountered in northern Maine by designing the base runway to extend 6 feet deep. Note the bombers in the background.[8]

Loring AFB parking apron with a B-52 in the foreground and KC-97 Stratofreighter aerial refueling tankers in the background, 1956.[9]

A nose hanger with a B-52 tail section protruding from within sits starkly against the stormy skies and snow-covered ground at Loring AFB.[10]

According to the air force, the Omaha Trophy is awarded to "units who demonstrate the highest standards in supporting the strategic deterrence mission." The 42nd Bombardment Wing was awarded the trophy in March 1978 for its strategic excellence during 1977.[11]

Right: Construction of the Loring Air Force Base flight control tower addition, located along the center of the flightline, November 1961.[12]

Below: Base housing in the late 1950s to early 1960s. One thing that stands out service-wide, on all bases in all branches, is the uniformity of base housing.[13]

Aerial photograph of partial Loring flightline showing the double-cantilever hangar at left foreground with the alert apron visible in the background, dated January 18, 1968.[14]

The interior of the double-cantilever hanger looking toward the center of the structure where the three-story maintenance shop structures are located.[15]

A KC-135 Stratotanker, all-jet refueling aircraft on the tarmac. Loring was strategically ideal for tankers to intercept aircraft flying over the North Atlantic.[16]

The sign that used to sit at the main entrance of the base. This sign no longer stands and visitors are now greeted with a Loring Commerce Center sign.[17]

4

NORTH RIVER DEPOT (CARIBOU AFS)

After dropping the Mk. III device on Nagasaki, the production of atomic weapons in the United States began in earnest: the only limitations being the slow advancement of fusion technologies and congressional budgeting at the time.

In creating an atomic bomb, the U.S. created a worldwide existential threat; with that power came the responsibility of maintaining the peace by acquiring and stockpiling weapons of mass destruction. To ensure that peace was maintained, it was concluded that the U.S. needed to provide a military deterrent of great strength, strategy, and armaments. It was the position of the USAF to promote peace with the promise of war. A position best summarized by General Thomas D. White, who stated: "effective deterrence includes the possession of military forces to deter war and, should war occur, the military strength to prevail."[1]

From its inception in the newly formed air force, SAC went through significant growing pains as it concentrated on its mission, its personnel, and training. However, by 1949, SAC commander General Lemay (who had played an important role in strategic bombardment during World War II) had developed SAC into a formidable atomic deterrence force which maintained a state of constant operational readiness. By the 1950s, the air force was greatly expanded. The B-52 and KC-135, all jet bomber and tanker (respectively), came into production, and General Lemay had instituted a rigorous training regimen to keep personnel in a state of constant operational readiness.

By 1950, the national weapons stockpile was growing exponentially, and concerns were being raised to increase the nation's stockpile storage locations. When weapons were offloaded from an aircraft, they would be taken to one of four top-secret stockpile sites where they would be inspected, serviced, and stored for future use. The logistics of handling and storing atomic weapons was becoming problematic and the need to be more operationally ready brought the concept of operational storage sites into focus.

Atomic weapons needed to be assembled, their components tested, and then disassembled with each use. The personnel that handled these weapons were highly trained specialists and the methods with which weapons had to be stored required rigid adherence to protocol. The Armed Forces Special Weapons Project (AFSWP) at the Sandia Corporation of Albuquerque, New Mexico, were responsible for the handling and safety of the weapons, as well as training personnel to handle the devices.

In 1950, the AFSWP allocated funds for the development of an operational storage facility in the northeast corner of the new air force base which was undergoing construction in Limestone, Maine. This facility would be the first and largest operational storage facility built in the U.S. It was to serve as a forward defensive position and distribution point for a variety of weapons in the U.S. arsenal to be utilized by the United States Air Force (SAC), the U.S. Navy, and others.

The site became partly operational in late 1951, but it was not until April 1952 when the construction was finished. North River Depot became fully operational in late summer when the 3080th Aviation Depot Group was ready for full operations. The infrastructure of the depot was a miniaturized version of the air force base next door. Recreational facilities, personnel living quarters (barracks), administrative areas, a weapons storage area (containing twenty-eight igloos and other storage structures), and bomb assembly plants were all included in the construction. On September 16, 1953, the weapons storage area was renamed Caribou Air Force Station.

Special weapons operational stockpiles were essential for the air force to be able to work in a nuclear environment while launching a sustained attack and it had also become essential for the U.S. to distribute its growing stockpile to operational areas. By 1955, the national stockpile consisted of 2,280 atomic and thermonuclear weapons and their distribution varied in accordance with mission and national security requirements. Weapons would arrive at Caribou Air Force Station by both rail and cargo planes arriving at nearby Loring.

Thermonuclear hydrogen bombs, atomic bombs, short-range attack missiles, and nuclear warheads were all stored and serviced at the site. Because of its function as an operational storage facility, nuclear weapons were continually being transported through the base. In addition to the weapons that the resident bombardment wing required to stay operational, the North River Depot was also a staging and storage facility for weapons being transported to operational forward areas throughout Europe.[2]

Assembly plants only lasted a short time as evolving bomb technology required less assembly and testing of thermonuclear weapons. In 1962, following a review of weapons storage and maintenance programs, the Atomic Energy Commission transferred ownership of the Caribou Air Force Station to SAC, allowing the military to assume control of the United States' deliverable weapons inventory. The responsibility of handling munitions was transferred from the 3080th Aviation Depot Group to the 42nd Bombardment Wing's 23rd Munitions Maintenance Squadron.

From 1951 until 1962, the North River Depot operated the first and largest operational nuclear storage facility in the U.S. The unsung heroes of the 3080th lived and worked in secrecy for more than a decade as they secured the safety of the U.S. by maintaining a nuclear arsenal that was ready to deploy at a moment's notice anywhere in the world in the protection of the United States' homeland, its territories, allies, and assets.

The short history of the North River Depot is filled with controversy, clandestine operations, and intrigue. Most of the activities that took place at the depot were shrouded in secrecy. The entire site was classified "Top Secret" until the Berlin Wall came down and the Cold War ended.

The 1962 closure of Caribou Air Force Station was merely a formality as the munition's storage and weapon's facilities of the Caribou Air Force Station were still very much in operation. A new page in the U.S. nuclear program had been turned. Thermonuclear weapons were lighter, more destructive, and more "turnkey" to operate, requiring far less hands-on maintenance.

A 1960s aerial photo of the North River Depot, aka Caribou Air Force Station. The weapons storage area (operational weapons stockpile) in its entirety can be seen in this image.[3]

The Q area was yet another name for Caribou Air Force Station, a name which goes back to its early planning stages. This was the command-and-control building for the Q area, part of the original Caribou Air Force Station, *c.* 1957.[4]

Above left: Interior door in the plutonium storage area, building 272. It is obvious how secure the area had to be when dealing with highly volatile, radioactive substances. The expertise of those who worked here is the reason no significant accidents or mishaps occurred. Photo from 1997, after declassification of the area.[5]

Above right: One of the plutonium storage vaults located in building 272. The cubicles shown in the interior of the vault was where "birdcages" containing plutonium were stored. Photo from 1997, after declassification of the area.[6]

Under the watchful eye of heavily armed security officers, a nuclear device is being loaded onto a bomber at Loring Air Force Base.[7]

5
LORING ALERT FORCE

Soviet technology was keeping pace with that of the U.S. who had lost their monopoly on atomic technology in 1949 when Russia detonated their first atomic bomb. On November 1, 1952, the U.S. introduced the hydrogen bomb to the world and the thermonuclear weapon was born. The new bomb, 1,000 times more powerful than the bomb dropped on Hiroshima, set a brisk pace for the arms race with the USSR trailing close behind the U.S.; Russia introduced their own thermonuclear technology less than a year later, on August 8, 1953.

Then the USSR began to pull ahead in the race. On August 21, 1957, Russia successfully tested the world's first intercontinental ballistic missile. Suddenly, the U.S. (who had been developing their own ICBM technology) was falling behind. Less than two months later, the USSR would launch the world's first orbiting satellite (Sputnik) on October 4, 1957.

With the Soviet Union's new advancements, Strategic Air Command determined that the response time for air force crews to get into the air must be lessened significantly to increase survivability. It was further determined the SAC war plan should be revised so that 33 percent of all available SAC aircraft would be operationally ready on a twenty-four-hour alert status. One-third of all SAC aircraft was to be loaded, fueled, prepped, and ready to take off at the sound of a klaxon in an around-the-clock state of readiness.

In October 1957, SAC established an alert force at Loring AFB. By January 1958, six B-52 bombers were on full alert, and the following June, three KC-135s were added. Initially, SAC required crews to be able to respond and have aircraft in the air within an hour's time. With new threats from the Soviet Union, and a new war plan from SAC, crews needed to have aircraft in the air within a fifteen-minute window, which was the predicted detection-to-detonation time of a Soviet ICBM strike.[1]

The twenty-four-hour nuclear alert began a period of maximum expenditures, worldwide tensions, and national fears as planes loaded with nuclear weapons maintained a constant state of readiness that would last for decades. As residents of Maine and Aroostook County enjoyed holidays, vacations, and went about their daily lives, B-52s loaded with weapons of mass destruction (WMDs) were prepped and loaded, on the tarmac and constantly ready to go in a moment's notice.

To ensure that alert crews maintained the optimal state of readiness, alert facilities, or "mole holes" were established to support the crews. Mole holes were windowless two-story installations with one story built underground. Alert facilities were built to accommodate different size alert crews, depending on the base and its requirements. At Loring AFB/Caribou AFS, the alert area was built in 1959 to accommodate seventy alert crew personnel.[2]

Inside the facilities, accommodations allowed for personnel to train, work, and relax within the security of the underground mole hole. When the alarm klaxon sounded, alert crews would jump into action and proceed to the awaiting B-52s, loaded with WMDs and standing by on the nearby alert apron, or "Christmas tree."

B-47 Stratojet bombers on alert at Loring. Stratojet bomber groups were typically assigned to forward bases worldwide on temporary assignment for a period of three months. Beginning in 1957, the Reflex Action program placed the bombers on three-week rotations. On November 22, 1958, a B-47 experienced a catastrophic crash upon takeoff at Loring AFB; all four crewmen were killed in the incident.

6

WEAPONS OF MASS DESTRUCTION

The Cold War produced many nuclear weapons, and the intensity of the arms buildup created a mutually assured destruction between the Soviet Union and United States. This mutually assured destruction, or MAD, was often thought to be the sole deterrent for a nuclear war between the two world superpowers. This created decades of anxiety as an entire generation grew up anticipating a nuclear incursion and witnessing the Cold War in all forms of media in popular culture. The novel *Planet of the Apes* was written by Pierre Boule and adopted into a screenplay. Movies such as *Red Dawn* and *War Games* (which featured Loring AFB), and even music ("99 Red Ballons" by Nena) made an entire generation acutely aware of the nuclear anxiety created between the two nations.

It is true that nearly everyone is aware of the Cold War and the billions of dollars' worth of infrastructure that was built and essentially never used, but what of the weapons? The buildup was astounding, and even more impressive when written out. So, here is a list of some of the weapons that went through Loring AFB/Caribou AFS, along with the history and specifications of each weapon.

The Mk. III, a 10,000-pound plutonium implosion bomb, nicknamed "Fatman." This extremely large bomb had a 21-kiloton yield and was used on Nagasaki, Japan. The bomb was produced from 1947–1949, and 120 of them were made.

The Mk. 6 was produced from 1951–1955 and weighed 8,500 pounds. This early plutonium device had a 40-kiloton yield (twice that of Nagasaki) and 1,100 of them were produced between 1951 and 1955. Another weapon was the Mk. 17, the heaviest nuclear device in the U.S. arsenal, weighing upwards of 42,000 pounds. This device had a yield of 10 to 15 megatons and 200 were made between 1956 and 1957.

The first lightweight hydrogen (thermonuclear) device was the Mk. 15, which weighed 7,600 pounds and had a 3.8 megaton yield. A total of 1,200 of these bombs were produced from 1955–1957. The Mk. 21 was another thermonuclear device with a 4.5-megaton yield. It was produced between 1955 and 1960, and 275 of them were manufactured. Another thermonuclear device, the Mk. 36, was a 10-megaton bomb which was made between 1956 and 1958; 940 were produced.

From 1962–1968, 700 Mk. 39 devices were made. These bombs had a yield of 40 megatons. The Mk. 41 was a 25-megaton bomb that weighed 10,000 pounds, and from

1960–1962, 500 of them were produced. The B-43 was a variable yield device (970 kt–1 mt) and 2,000 of them were produced from 1959–1965. The Mk. 53 was a 9-megaton device and 350 were produced between 1962 and 1965.

Other nuclear devices at Loring were thermonuclear-tipped warheads. The short-range attack missile, the AGM 69-A, was equipped with a W-69, 200-kiloton warhead. Between 1971 and 1976, 1,500 of them were produced. Finally, the Hound Dog missile was equipped with a W-28 thermonuclear warhead with a 70-kiloton to 1.45-megaton yield; 900 were produced before 1966.

This is a list of nuclear devices that were present at Loring rather than conventional weapons. Loring saw its fair share of both, and it is almost certain that other nuclear weapons passed through Loring or were stored at Caribou Air Force Station and are not listed here. It is not meant to be a complete list, but instead a study of the magnitude and severity of the nuclear arms stockpile in Maine.

The nuclear program in the U.S. was robust from start to finish during the Cold War. The evolution of these weapons went from primitive to sophisticated in less than a decade. The early weapons were very cumbersome, heavy, and required exacting hands-on preparation. As thermonuclear technology evolved, weapons became more reliable, more powerful, and smaller. Despite the smaller size of modern nuclear weapons, they yield considerably more power than their early atomic predecessors, and they can be delivered with much more accuracy.

The Mk. III or "Fatman" atomic bomb. This is like the one detonated over Nagasaki and was an early plutonium fission device.[1]

An Mk. 15 thermonuclear device. Although it was not related to activities at Loring AFB, an Mk. 15 was involved in a "broken arrow" incident when it was jettisoned from a B-47 over Tybee Island, following a mid-air collision with an F-86 on February 5, 1958. The 7,600-pound bomb remains missing, presumably at the bottom of Wassaw Sound off the coast of Tybee Island in Georgia.[2, 3]

A trailer-mounted Hound Dog missile (AGM-28) passes by during the 1961 inaugural parade for President John F. Kennedy.[4]

Members of the 42nd Munitions Maintenance Squadron load an Mk. 60 CAPTOR (encapsulated torpedo) anti-submarine mine onto a 42nd Bombardment Wing B-52G.[5]

7
IN DEFENSE OF LORING

In the late 1940s, Soviet technology and weaponry advances were creating a new sense of urgency for the military, but the public was not convinced, and military budget restraints had been slowing the arms buildup. Then, when the conflict in Korea began in June 1950, the public became much more aware of current events, much more fearful of the spread of communism, and much more willing to commit money to military purses.

The air force knew it needed to strengthen a nuclear defensive position to deter the Soviet Union from attack, but it also realized that our positions needed to be protected, not just by the air force, but by the army and the North American Air Defense Command (NORAD, est. 1957). To create a solid line of defense in coordination with the army, and other services, the air force developed its Air Defense Command (ADC; reactivated 1951) and worked to coordinate a solid line of early warning detection and response/intercept teams in defense of an anticipated Soviet attack.

Strategic Air Command was still three years away from having an operational base and in response to the growing urgent need to protect SAC assets, as well as the infrastructure of the U.S., the army formed the Army Anti-Aircraft Command (ARAACOM) in July 1950. In the next decade, the command would grow exponentially and become part of a "vast air defense network that included supersonic jet fighters, antiaircraft guns and missiles, radars of all varieties, hundreds of information-passing nodes, and tens of thousands of soldiers, airmen, sailors and civilians ... established to counter the anticipated Soviet bomber threat."[1] Anti-aircraft battalions evolved into over 200 missile bases peaking with over 40,000 personnel stationed throughout the county. Each would be set up in defense of capital areas, ports of industry, weapons production factories, and SAC bases, such as the one being built in Limestone.

Army anti-aircraft (AAA) battalions then began to activate in different high-target probability areas using surplus World War II 90-mm and 120-mm guns, as well as the new 75-mm Skysweeper, which represented the latest in radar-tracked automatic weaponry. The Skysweeper could destroy enemy targets in flight as far as 4 miles away, and it could detect approaching enemy aircraft from 15 miles away. Firing a cyclic forty-five rounds per minute, it was a fully capable weapon for stopping enemy aircraft.

The Skysweeper was quickly replaced by the Nike Ajax missile. However, before the Nike missile bases began to activate around Limestone to defend the B-52 Stratofortress airfield, the 548th AAAW Skysweeper Battalion was there until September 1, 1958. The Skysweeper battalion at Limestone was one of only eight AW battalions active in the U.S. at the peak of the weapon's use in the mid-1950s (when it was replaced by the NIKE missile).[2]

In September 1957, four Nike missile launch facilities were activated in the defense of Loring AFB. The Nike missile was a surface-to-air anti-aircraft missile, and it was the result of years of development and research which began in 1945 when Bell Telephone Labs started Project Nike, named after the Greek goddess of victory.

Originally named the SAM-A7 (surface-to-air missile, seventh design), it was later named the Nike Ajax, and it was capable of hitting a high-altitude target traveling at supersonic speeds. The missile was fired from a fixed position on the ground, or in most cases, raised and fired from an underground horizontal storage silo. It was controlled and launched at separate facilities, usually located within a mile of each other. The control facility would use radar to track both the targets and outgoing missiles. Nike sites activated to defend Loring were designated L-13, L-31, L-58, and L-85, located in Caswell, Limestone, Caribou, and Connor respectively. One battalion controlled all four of the Nike sites around Loring, and it was the U.S. Army's 3rd Missile Battalion which manned these Nike sites.

Site L-31 was the most short-lived of the three. It was only in service for a year and was deactivated in September 1958. Both the L-13 and L-58 sites converted from Nike Ajax missiles to Nike Hercules in 1960. Like their namesake Greek heroes, the Hercules was more powerful than the Ajax missile. The Nike Hercules could climb 100,000 feet and travel at Mach 4. Its operational range was 90 miles, three times that of the Ajax's 30-mile range. The most fearsome thing about this brute of a missile was its warhead; in addition to conventional warheads, the Nike Hercules could be armed with either a Mk. 97 or Mk. 22 thermonuclear warhead, the missile could deliver either a 2- or 20-kiloton punch to its target, vaporizing it in the air as it approached.

By the mid-1960s, ICBM technology (along with its early-warning detection systems and advanced anti-missile weapons) had rendered the Nike obsolete. In addition, the bomber mission had changed, and the U.S. no longer had to fear incoming Soviet long-range bombers, but instead incoming ICBMs were becoming the universal concern. The remaining three U.S. Army 3rd Missile Battalion Nike missile sites that had protected Loring AFB since 1958 were deactivated in June 1966.

During this period of the Cold War, the services all formed a close working relationship with one another. The Department of Defense (DOD), air force, army, NORAD, and others all worked together to impede or prevent attacks on U.S. soil by the Soviet Union. In that spirit, the Vandenburg-Collins agreement was signed on August 1, 1950, by Army Chief of Staff General J. Lawton Collins, and Air Force Chief of Staff Gen. Hoyt S. Vandenburg. The agreement outlined how both the ARAACOM and USAF ADC would integrate their defense capabilities against a common enemy with the air force maintaining a defense posture for the U.S. and the army defending air force assets and U.S. airspace.[3]

The M51 Skysweeper was an 8,750-pound, radar-controlled machine-gun with an effective radar range of 18.5 miles and a vertical shooting range of 30,000 feet. The gun was a mobile weapon mounted on wheels or "bogies" which had to be removed before outriggers would secure the gun into a static firing position.[4]

Nike missile site PH 07L in Richboro, PA., with four Nike Ajax missiles locked into firing position. Image by MSGT Robert J. Grey, October 1959. Although this site is not in Maine, the layout of all Nike bases was similar.[5]

Above: A Nike Ajax missile launch site with open silo access doors and decontamination shower in the foreground. The Nike Ajax missiles pictured are in the horizontal position as they would appear when elevated from the underground silo, before being raised and locked into the firing position.[6]

Left: A Nike Hercules missile raised and locked into the firing position. Photo taken during Project 26 testing in Hawaii, 1962.[7]

8

CASWELL AFS

Once the Korean War opened the public's collective eye to the foreign affairs of the country and current events in the world, military expenditures became robust. Aside from the obvious military hardware, the United States' reinforcement of its detection, warning, and communication systems were as important as the weapons and infrastructure buildup. When you consider that weapons cannot be deployed against an enemy if that enemy is not first detected, then methods of early detection become paramount. To defend a country, the enemy must first be identified and tracked, and as United States' guidance and detection systems became more advanced, they became more prominent, and their use was essential in the defense of the U.S. and North America. In 1950, as construction was being expedited on military projects across the country, the Caswell Air Force Station was built in Caswell, Maine.

The Caswell AFS was an aircraft control and warning station that became operational in 1951. Its radars scanned the airspace of the Loring Defense Area, searching for incoming enemy aircraft. The station was also part of a vast network of early warning radar lines throughout North America. The Pine Tree Line, Mid-Canada Line, and Distant Early Warning Line were all set up to detect incoming Soviet long-range bombers approaching North America from the Arctic Circle.

Caswell AFS served as a ground-control intercept (GCI) and early warning station until 1959 when the station joined the semi-automatic ground environment (SAGE). Russia's accomplishments in atomic technology had been catching up with that of the United States', and with the announcement that the Russians had developed long-range bomber technology, a new sense of urgency had created a need to protect the skies from oncoming threats, and the SAGE network would do just that.

The SAGE system was an automated system that would send an initial alert to a direction center, which would relay information to combat centers, alert interceptor aircraft, and anti-aircraft weapons to target the incoming threat. It was an elaborate system developed by Lincoln Laboratory at the Massachusetts Institute of Technology (MIT), and at the time of its inception and activation it was cutting edge technology. As MIT explains it:

> A large network of radars would automatically detect a hostile bomber formation as it approached the U.S. mainland from any direction. The radar detections would be

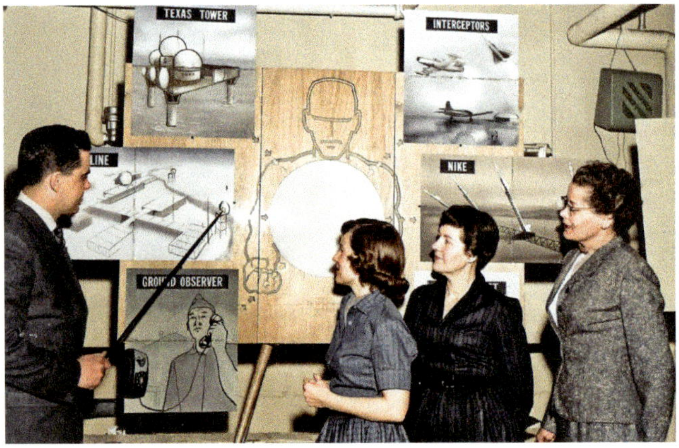

A representative from *New England Telephone and Telegraph* conducts a lecture explaining the semi-automatic ground environment system at an unnamed Maine college, *circa* 1958.[1]

> transmitted over telephone lines to the nearest SAGE direction center, where they would be processed by an AN/FSQ-7 computer. The direction center would then send out notification and continuous targeting information to the air bases best situated to carry out interception of the approaching bombers, as well as to a set of surface-to-air missile batteries.[2]

The 766th Radar Squadron (formally 766 Aircraft Control and Warning Squadron) was assigned to the base, and during the Nike era, the army occupied the base as well. In 1980, the station was deactivated, not long before ADC's deactivation in 1980 when its assets were divided between SAC and Tactical Air Command (TAC).

1292nd Airways and Air Communications Service Squadron

Emergency action messages, troop movements, weather reports, surveillance, and ship-to-shore (or aircraft-to-land) communications are just some of the forms of electronic communication used by the U.S. military. Even though all these forms of communication vary, they all have one thing in common: they generate or terminate from one of the vast communication centers located within the military infrastructure.

The 1292nd Airways and Air Communications Service Squadron was designated and organized on July 15, 1955, and at the same time in 1955, a communications annex was constructed in Perham, about 22 miles from Limestone. The squadron was located at the annex, primarily operating a high-frequency global communications system (GLOBECOM) used to communicate with flight traffic, naval assets, and alternate stations. The network was also often used for telephone communications via the Defense Switched Network (DSN) between air traffic and ground locations. The Perham location served as a transmitter station and the receiving station was located nearer to Loring, just outside of its west gate access road.

In July 1961, the 1292nd AACS Squadron was redesignated the 2192nd Communications Squadron when it relocated to Loring Air Force Base. In 1962, the Perham Communications annex was closed. Communication remains the backbone of the Air Force, and the duties are now handled by the 42nd Communications Squadron which was designated on November 1, 2009.

CHANGE 2 UNCLASSIFIED 2-50o

ADMINISTRATIVE PLANNING CRITERIA AND PROCEDURES

UNCLASSIFIED NAVSHIPS 92675

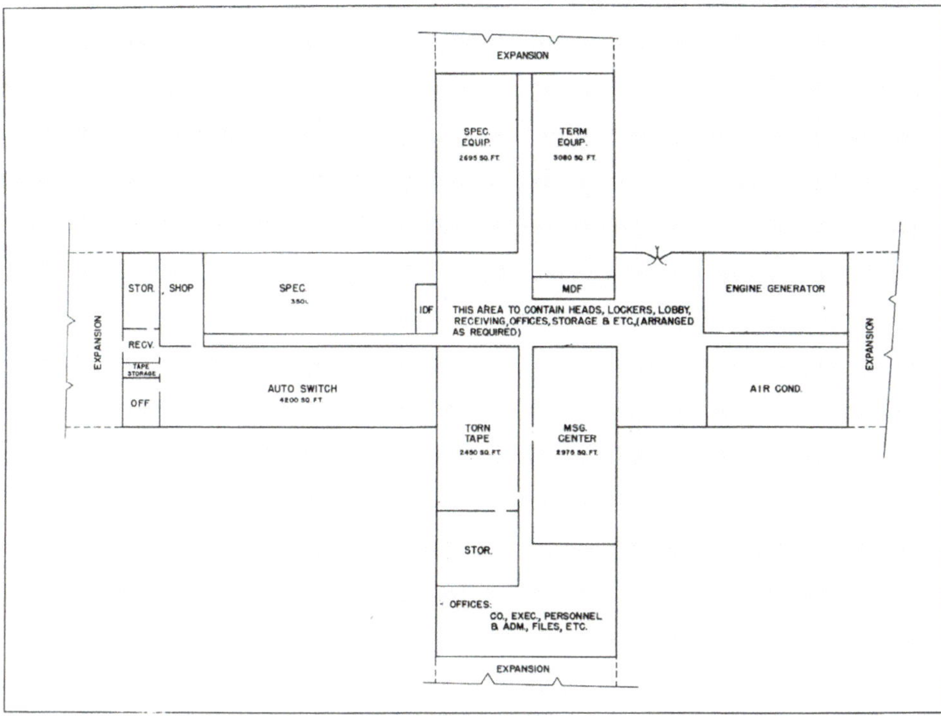

Figure 2-19

Figure 2-19 Proposed Typical Layout for Communication Center

Above : The curious shape of the communications center in Perham was done by design and was part of administrative planning and procedure. The architectural design was a common layout of military communication centers at the time.

Below: The situation room or war room. Communication here was essential as leaders gathered to continually monitor exercises and operational movements. The boards on the walls would allow commanders to keep track of who was assigned to each task and the curtains to the right of the picture are covering windows to a room where communication specialists constantly relayed real-time information to the leadership in the room. The clocks on the table used to adorn the walls and were set to different global time zones. (*2024 Panoramic photo courtesy of Charles Cormier*)

9

PRESQUE ISLE AFB

On January 12, 1948, the air force activated the dormant Presque Isle Army Airfield and redesignated it the Presque Isle Air Force Base. From its activation, and for the majority of the 1950s, the base was assigned to the Air Defense Command (ADC). The 23rd Fighter-Interceptor Wing dominated the base from 1950–1952, and from 1952–1955, the 74th, 75th, 57th, 82nd, 76th, and 318th Fighter-Interceptor Squadrons all rotated through the base.

On August 18, 1955, the 23rd Fighter Wing was activated at Presque Isle AFB. Before being deactivated on July 1, 1959, both the 75th and 76th Fighter Squadrons flew Northrop F-89 Scorpions from the base at Presque Isle. The mission of the fighter-interceptor squadrons was to provide air defense of the continental United States (CONUS) in the event of a Soviet long-range bomber incursion.

The main gate of Presque Isle Air Force Base during the Air Defense Command, fighter-interceptor era. (*Oscar "Voscar" Nelder photo. Reproduced from the collection of Dr. Richard Graves, used by permission*)

A Snark missile once decorated the landscape displaying admiration and pride in Strategic Air Command's short-lived Snark missile base. (*Oscar "Voscar" Nelder photo. Reproduced from the collection of Dr. Richard Graves, used by permission*)

10
SNARKS: ICMS

The nation's first intercontinental cruise missile (ICM) was the ill-fated SM-62 Snark, which was a surface-to-surface missile launched from a mobile launch device. The Snark could carry a 3.8-megaton W39 thermonuclear warhead, had a maximum range of approximately 5,500 miles, and could travel at a top speed of nearly 650 miles per hour. The missiles were notoriously unreliable, and a Strategic Missile Evaluation Committee considered the Snark program unsatisfactory in 1954. During a test flight in December 1956, a Snark launched from Florida failed to respond to control efforts and went missing; its last verified sighting was as it was heading toward the jungles of Brazil. The missile was not recovered until 1982 when a Brazilian farmer discovered it. The missile was so unreliable that people began to joke that the waters off the coast of Florida were "Snark infested waters" due to the amount of failed test flights.[1]

Despite this, SAC activated the 556th Strategic Missile Squadron in December 1957 and began training with Snark missiles. Despite the bad reputation and short lifespan of the Snark missile program, it was a very important weapon in the Cold War as it was an important step in the development of the intercontinental ballistic missile (ICBM) which both immediately succeeded the Snark and was the reason for the Snark's rapid retirement.

The only active Snark launch facility in the world was located at Presque Isle AFB and was active for less than four months before the Snark missile program was mothballed and the weapon was declared obsolete. The 67-foot-long missile had a wingspan of 42 feet and weighed 48,000 pounds. It was transported by a trailer which also served as its launching platform. When not in use, missiles were stored in strategic hangars located adjacent to the launch pads.

On January 1, 1959, SAC activated the 702nd Strategic Missile Wing (ICM-Snark) at Presque Isle AFB. Its first Snark was placed on alert in March 1960, but the unit did not achieve combat-ready status until February 28, 1961, only to have the entire program scraped and the 702nd Missile Wing deactivated on June 25, 1961. After the 702nd was deactivated, "the Air Force disposed of $141,000,000 in supplies and excess equipment."[2]

After the departure of the ADC in 1959, the air force had turned the flightline over to the City of Presque Isle, and after the departure of SAC in June 1961, the air force left Presque Isle altogether. On December 15, 1961, the air force turned ownership and control of the remainder of the base over to the City of Presque Isle.

A Snark missile being unloaded from an air force transport plane at Presque Isle. (*Oscar "Voscar" Nelder photo. Reproduced from the collection of Dr. Richard Graves, used by permission*)

The Snark shown on its transport trailer/launch platform. The truck is bringing it to the launch pad adjacent to the missile hangar. (*Oscar "Voscar" Nelder photo. Reproduced from the collection of Dr. Richard Graves, used by permission*)

The Snark missile being made ready to fire. This was presumably a training exercise that took place to demonstrate base preparedness. (*Oscar "Voscar" Nelder photo. Reproduced from the collection of Dr. Richard Graves, used by permission*)

The missile is being raised into its firing position. At this point, the missile and its armed warhead would be locked into its firing position and launched at its target. (*Oscar "Voscar" Nelder photo. Reproduced from the collection of Dr. Richard Graves, used by permission*)

11

AFTER THE ICBM

The 1960s did not ease world tensions in the slightest. The Far East brought the world a sense of *déjà vu* when the U.S. went to war in Asia to fight communism again, this time in Vietnam. However, it was not southeast Asia, it was an island in the Caribbean Sea that contributed the most to the Cold War.

In October 1962, President John F. Kennedy announced that reconnaissance aircraft revealed the construction of Soviet nuclear missile launch facilities in Cuba. Strategic Air Command set Defcon II for the first time on October 24, 1962. The tensions in the U.S. were at an all-time high. A potential installation in Cuba would challenge United States' strategic defenses due to the island being to the south and all the radar arrays being oriented to the Arctic Circle. A missile base in Cuba would directly threaten multiple SAC bomber bases, naval bases, and the entire eastern seaboard. In addition to U.S. naval blockades, SAC increased the size of its alert force to one-half the entire force, placing aircraft from Loring and other U.S. bases on twenty-four-hour airborne alert with more than fifty U.S. bombers continuously patrolling various parts of the globe, loaded with nuclear weapons. The show of force was unsuccessful in curtailing the Russian plans in Cuba, and it only seemed to provoke things more. War seemed inevitable, but Russia backed away from its Cuban missile plans after Soviet premier Nikita Khrushchev and President Kennedy conducted clandestine talks, with the latter conceding to the removal of United States' Jupiter missiles in Turkey.

However, that did not stop the arms race. Both the U.S. and the Soviet Union continued developing, testing, and producing weapons, weapons technology, and other military assets in effort to ascertain world dominance, or secure world peace (depending on your perspective).

Hound Dog missiles arrived at Loring in 1960, and by the end of the following year, crews had integrated the weapon into their arsenal and were fully trained and operationally ready for the missiles to be utilized in the alert force. Armed with a thermonuclear-tipped warhead, Hound Dog missiles gave SAC the ability of guided missile strikes by using bombers to penetrate Russian airspace. Each B-52 could carry two Hound Dog missiles, one on each side, mounted underneath its wings. Used in conjunction with the Quail decoy missile, the Hound Dog revolutionized bomber-delivered nuclear weapons. For thirteen years, the Hound Dog was kept in service, and it was removed from alert forces in 1975. A small number of them remained in stockpile storage and the last missile was scrapped from Loring AFB in 1978.[1]

The replacement for the Hound Dog was the AGM-69 SRAM (short-range attack missile). Coincidentally, before Loring held the last Hound Dog missile in weapons storage, it was the first SAC base to have operational B-52s equipped with SRAM delivery systems in mid-1972. Also in 1972, teams from Loring participated in the conventional bombing campaign in Southeast Asia code-named Linebacker II during the month of December, dropping over 20,000 tons of ordinance on Vietnam. The campaign was the largest military offensive involving heavy bombers to have occurred since World War II. One of Loring's bombers was struck by antiaircraft fire over North Vietnam during the campaign, but the crew survived after bailing out of the disabled aircraft over Thailand.

In the late 1970s, talks of nuclear reductions became more of a one-side attempt when Russia developed the mid-range SS-20 mobile ballistic missile, creating an immediate threat to allied European nations. Buildup in the Soviet Union continued, and they began expanding their military presence in Africa and the Middle East before finally invading Afghanistan. All the while, the U.S. faced military budget cutbacks and force reductions.

The 1980s ushered in change as President Ronald Reagan vowed to continue the buildup of American military strength. The new commander-in-chief was a staunch opponent of communism and very vocal about his distrust of the Soviet Union. His administration opined that the cutbacks had weakened the country, and the then-Defense Secretary Casper Weinberger stated he believed that the USSR sought world domination and would not stop at nuclear war to get it. The philosophy of deterrence through strength was once again a prominent philosophy with U.S. armed forces.[2]

After some weakening in the late 1970s, it seemed the arms race was back on. However, as it would turn out, the decade of '80s was to come in like a lion and go out like a lamb with its threat of nuclear holocaust. In the early 1980s, the Loring alert force was still maintaining its around-the-clock vigil of peacekeeping through nuclear deterrence. In the book *The History of Loring Air Force Base*, author and air force veteran Victor Kraft outlines the use of nuclear weapons at Loring, and states that four B-52s were always on alert during the 1980s, armed with "eight SRAMS (200 kiloton) and two Mk-53 (9 megatons yield) at least."[3]

In addition to the continuing nuclear alert, the 1980s were brisk with conventional warfare training as well. Improvements were made to many of the facilities around Loring and $3.5 million was spent on the runway alone, first on a taxiway project in 1981 and then the construction of a second runway in 1985. Upon completion of the second runway, which was parallel to the first, bombers and refuelers could take-off simultaneously on the opposing runways, increasing efficiency and response time. In the '80s, everything seemed to be business as usual at Loring AFB; then the year 1987 brought radical change.

President Ronald Reagan visited the Berlin Wall, and the old-school "kill the Commies" mindset became a mind bent on peace. Russian leader Mikhail Sergeyevich Gorbachev had been relaxing Russia's grip on other countries in the Eastern Bloc. Hungary and Poland were making unobstructed strides toward free elections, and the

Soviet military pulled out of Afghanistan. Then, in a pivotal moment of the Cold War, President Ronald Reagan visited the Berlin Wall on June 12, 1987. Erected in 1961, the Berlin Wall separated East and West Berlin, and it had become the unofficial monument to the Cold War. Standing at the wall's Brandenburg Gate, Reagan gave one of the most controversial and memorable speeches of his presidency. If Winston Churchill's Iron Curtain speech can be considered the opening volley of the Cold War, this speech is certainly a contender for its final blow. The final line of President Reagan's address was a call for immediate peace and signaled the end of decades of pent-up hostility between two nations:

> General Secretary Gorbachev, if you seek peace, if you seek prosperity for the Soviet Union and Eastern Europe, if you seek liberalization, come here to this gate.
>
> Mr. Gorbachev, open this gate!
>
> Mr. Gorbachev, tear down this wall![4]

Nuclear reduction talks, free elections in Eastern Bloc Countries, and economic reform all began to happen very quickly as President Reagan completed his final term in office. His successor, President George H. W. Bush, was residing at the White House when the wall came down on November 9, 1989. The world rejoiced for the future of Europe and the dissolution of the Cold War. During the Malta Summit between the United States and the Soviet Union in December, both countries shared an acknowledgement that the Cold War had come to an end with no clear winner, and no shots fired.

With the destruction of the Berlin Wall, a new sense of peace and hope was felt around the world as the Iron Curtain was lifted and the Soviet Union was dissolved. President Bush ordered the SAC bomber alert force to stand down in September 1991, after more than three decades of constant, around-the-clock nuclear readiness. Then, after New Years' Eve 1991, the Soviet Union ceased to exist.

To the dismay of Maine representatives and residents alike, and to the sheer horror of the residents of Aroostook County, Loring Air Force Base was selected for closure under by the Base Realignment and Closure Commission of 1991. Strategic Air Command was then deactivated on June 1, 1992, and the air force restructured, placing Loring under the command of the newly formed Air Combat Command (ACC).

However, Loring's fate was sealed, and on September 30, 1994, Strategic Air Command's first B-36 bomber base was closed after forty-one years of being one of the most heavily armed SAC bases in the nation and a key component of the Cold War.

A KC-135 Stratotanker can be seen in the background of the image as snow removal crews work to clear the runway.[5]

AGM-69 SRAMs loaded into the bomb bay of a B-52H along with two B-28 thermonuclear bombs, 1984.[6]

President Ronald Reagan speaks with an unidentified army security officer at Checkpoint Charlie in West Berlin, June 1982.[7]

President Ronald Reagan and Soviet General Secretary Mikhail Gorbachev sign the Intermediate-Range Nuclear Forces Treaty on December 8, 1987.[8]

12

THIRTY YEARS LATER

Although the U.S. Air Force was present in other parts of Maine during the Cold War, as were other branches of the armed forces, I selected Aroostook County for this book because of the significant impact the base has had on this region of Maine. In addition, not only was the infrastructure buildup tremendous, but it was the most elaborate, most costly, and the most technically challenging (from an engineering perspective) of any other Cold War buildup in the state of Maine.

The population and prosperity of the Limestone area saw a tremendous boom and bust, and the entirety of Aroostook County has been impacted if we analyze U.S. census statistics over the period of the Cold War. In Limestone, the population as Loring construction was underway in 1950 was at 2,427. The population grew 439 percent in the next decade to 13,102 in 1960. If we jump forward two decades, we arrive at 1980 following the cutbacks and reductions of the Carter administration; the population of Limestone was standing at 8,719 people. Another decade later in 1990, the U.S. and Russia had agreed to disarm nuclear weapons stockpiles following the Reagan buildup, the population was 9,922. Now, according to the 2020 census, the population of Limestone is somewhere near 1,526, even lower than the pre-World War II population of 1,855 residents in 1940. Aroostook County fared somewhat better because it has strong commercial centers in Houlton and Presque Isle, but nevertheless, in 1970 the population of Aroostook County was 94,100 residents, dropping to 66,800 in the 2020 census.

As I was writing this book, I was fortunate to have interviewed several residents of Aroostook County and spent some time riding around with my friend and tour guide Charlie who is in his seventh decade living in the County. He told me he could recall the fighter planes coming and going from Presque Isle when he was in his early school years. The teacher would have to stop teaching as they flew over due to the roar of the engines. Often, the children would cheer with glee if there were a sonic boom! Later in life, Charlie was a service industry technician with base access and spent many hours working on Loring AFB. Around town, he recalls there being several car dealerships, thriving appliance and department stores, brisk furniture sales, and bustling commerce everywhere that culminated with the grand opening of the Aroostook Center mall in 1993.

None of that exists now. Businesses are shuttered, entire neighborhoods are empty, a drive around some of the remaining Loring facilities reveal what you might envision a dystopian post-apocalyptic world would look like, and the Aroostook Center Mall failed to be sold at auction in 2017. Wells Fargo took over the property for $4 million, more than 90 percent under its appraised 2001 value.[1]

With the exception of the two L-58 sites in Caribou, the remaining Nike sites, communication center, and Caswell AFS are all now under private ownership. As the following photographic tour indicates, some surprisingly still resemble what they once were. Others have been integrated back into their communities, and more still are left crumbling and rusting while being reclaimed by nature. I had the privilege of speaking with some landowners as I was doing my research and some would like to preserve what they have, and others wish it would disappear completely so they could use their land without the hassle of removing the remnants.

This seems to be the case with many of the residents I spoke with. Some reminisce about the days of the jets and constant readiness, and others just want to get on with life in the County, but most people agree that the area could use some solid developmental growth.

The Loring Development Authority took over control of Loring in 1997 and is searching for something to fill the void that was left with the departure of Loring AFB, but as of the writing of this book, we are nearing the thirtieth anniversary of the closure of Loring, so the search has been long, and the void remains unfilled.

Some small areas of the former base have been repurposed by government agencies such as the United States Job Corp and the Defense Finance and Accounting Service, but large portions of the base are derelict, and some are in an advanced state of decay. The most recent attempt at injecting life into the base was Maine Military Authority, a state-run business that employed over 500 people at its peak. Failure to resolve a contract dispute resulted in the layoffs of its remaining workforce in 2018.

The Cold War is over. The planes, bombs, and personnel have all departed and all that remains are the rusting remnants of what once was. Four decades of uneasiness in an uncertain world is now evidenced by only ghosts, and the roar of jet engines is forever silent. It is often said that those who ignore history are doomed to repeat it, and it brings about the notion that a grave mistake is about to be made in letting these artifacts fade away. There will never be another arch hangar in Maine that was made for the B-36 bomber, nor will there ever be a specially designed airfield for the Cold War peacekeepers who silently and bravely protected our nation while citizens slept snuggly in their beds, unaware of the looming threat.

Perhaps it is time to consider the preservation of these historic places before it is too late. In a 1998 United States Air Force Official Historic Building Inventory and Evaluation of Loring Air Force base, the author writing on the behalf of the U.S. Air Force wrote:

> The built environment of Loring AFB, a primary component in the policy of containment and deterrence, demonstrates the military, technological, and economic complexity of the Cold War. Once one of the most heavily armed of the SAC bases, it stands as a visible representation of the policies that shaped the political, economic, and military history of the world.

The report goes on to state that the airfield, arch hangar, DC hangar, and alert area were all recommended for protection under the National Register of Historic places.[2]

These corrugated metal hangers held fighter-interceptor aircraft during the time the base was an active part of the Air Defense Command structure. Now they are utilized as commercial space at the Presque Isle International Airport.

One of the Snark missile hangers that are remnants of the Snark missile program and evidence of the only Snark missile base to ever exist.

The only thing that remains of the M51 Skysweeper gun emplacement are these two clumps of trees standing at the edge of a potato field with visibility for miles. Within the clumps are two decaying wooden structures. One was for crew members and the other was a power supply building.

The crew building was large enough for a couple of bunkbeds and a small sitting area. There was also a bathroom, refrigerator, and large water tank inside.

Location of Nike control site for L-31 launch facility in Limestone. There has been an addition placed on the original barracks building, but you can still see the air force-influenced architecture. The base has been repurposed and is now a bed and breakfast aptly named NIKE Acres.

On the hill behind NIKE Acres B&B stands two identical radar towers. They are partially obscured by foliage and standing in the tree line along the edge of a potato field.

The barracks building for the L-31 Nike launch facility in Limestone. Many of the original structures remain and the owner wishes to preserve them to the best of their ability.

Above left: Inside the barracks building which still has the original tile and color scheme. The building is in remarkable condition and needs only minor repairs.

Above right: Access doors to silo number three at the L-31 launch facility. Many of the other components (such as the emergency shower) are all long-gone. The current owner saved this whole silo containment area from being buried underneath a snowmobile and trailer junkyard.

Above left: Inside silo three. Doors above the bay would open and the missile would be raised up above ground before being vertically erected into a firing position and launched.

Above right: A different angle inside the silo. The missile bay becomes filled with water when the spring thaw floods the sixty-six-year-old silo, but the ground reclaims the water by late spring.

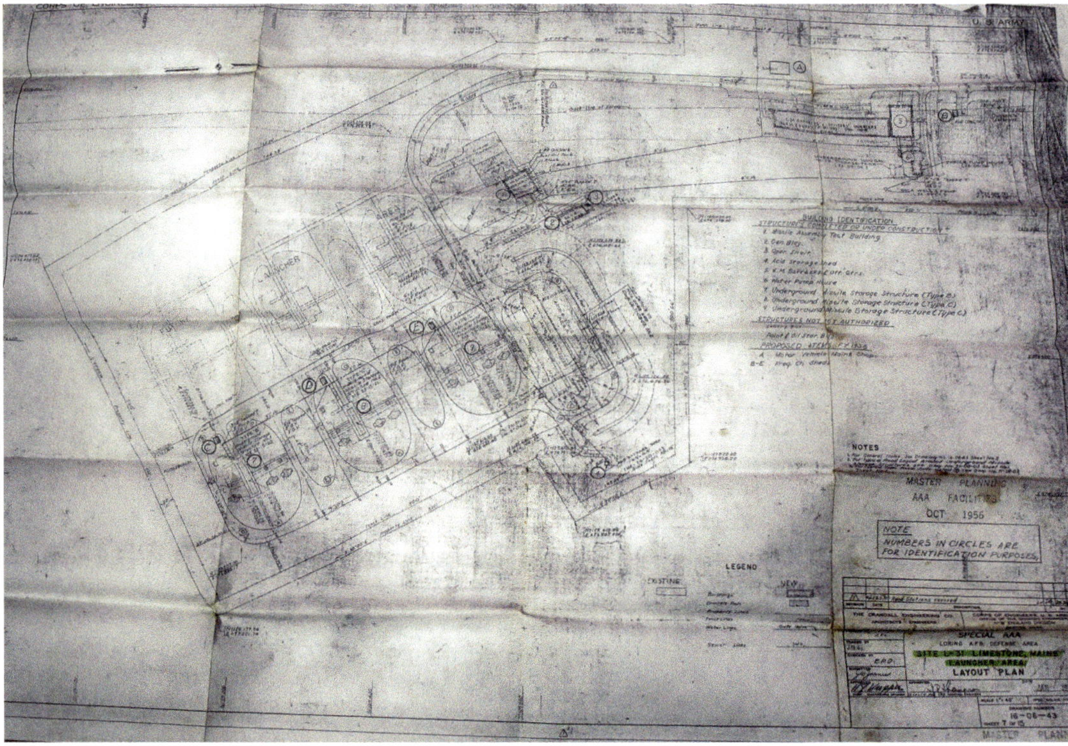

Above: The original construction blueprint for the L-31 Nike missile launch facility. The site owner has many fascinating documents from the early days of the Cold War.

Left: The unit insignia located inside the silo on the entrance wall has held up incredibly well in its underground location, protected from the sun and elements for sixty-six years and counting.

All that remains of the L-58 Nike launch facility is a dilapidated guard shack and four concrete sealed missile silos. The City of Caribou and its residents have been very successful at reclaiming old Nike sites and most of the evidence of their existence is gone.

If we turn and look away from the launch area, out past the crumbling guard shack, the only thing that reveals air force architecture is the chimney on the large red structure in the background; it was once the barracks building and it is now VFW post 9389. The buildings in the middle of the property are now a school for special needs students.

The L-58 control site location offers no indication that there was once a Nike radar installation here, but the property is still under federal ownership, and it is still a radar site. It is now part of the FAA long-range radar network which tracks air traffic at a range of 200 miles. It is also part of the Joint Surveillance System Network which shares data with the air force, NORAD, and other Homeland Security assets. This communication and radar data network replaced the SAGE network in 1983.

The L-85 launch facility barracks is in an advanced state of decay. The buildings at the site in Connor have suffered from many years of neglect.

Like the launch area in Caribou, the silo doors have been sealed with concrete, but unlike the launch site in Caribou, the buildings in Connor are facing imminent collapse.

Above left: The control site in Connor has suffered a much worse fate. All that remains are a few concrete foundations which are soon to be removed so the farmers can reclaim the area.

Above right: An access point to an underground area at the Connor control site is concealed in high brush, but the ladder goes nowhere, about four feet down is a solid dirt floor. Whatever was down there has been filled in.

The L-13 site in Caswell is probably the best example of what the original launch sites looked like. It even still has the dog kennels which is at the bottom center of the image. The buildings are unfortunately showing their age and the barracks is crumbling apart, but the property is currently being cared for by private owners.

The light-poles, gate houses, and fence line are all original and remain intact. The smaller outbuildings are in better shape than the barracks and the property is an impressive piece of Cold War history. As I mentioned earlier in the book, this was one of the two sites that converted to the nuclear-capable Hercules missile.

The L-13C site is as equally impressive as the launch site. All the components are there, fencing, guard shack, buildings. Even four radar towers remain standing on the property.

Up close, the site is in a very advanced state of decay. In this interior shot of the barracks, you can see the support beam for the roof is beginning to give way.

The large concrete towers looming in the north Maine woods seem out of place and it is hard to conceive the notion that men once worked here who anticipated a nuclear war each and every day.

Above left: This radar tower is in remarkable condition. It is uncertain why the other three are stripped of all hardware, yet this one remains like this.

Above right: All the abandoned installations and bases had paved roads into and around them at one time, but many of them are grown in and no longer resemble roads, like this one going into the Caswell control site.

The GLOBALCOM communications annex in Perham. Early military global communications technologies paved the way for modern day internet. Many conveniences we enjoy today like constant use of the Global Positioning System, or GPS, would not be possible if not for technological military advancements.

The communications annex is a curious design which resembles a cross from the air. The aerial shot also allows for a good view of the paved road that goes around the entire complex. The road is quickly returning to nature, and just outside of the image at top center, the road is blocked by a beaver who has built a damn and flooded a large section of the forest and road. The beaver is the reason I could not walk in and had to send up the drone.

The annex in Perham acted primarily as a transmission facility and for every transmission facility there had to be locations that acted as receivers. This is one such building and is located outside the west gate access road at Loring.

Caswell Air Force Station as it appears in June 2024. The property is owned by one of the area potato growers who uses the base area to store and maintain his equipment, and he rents out the old housing units.

One of the air force buildings that seems to get very little use. Each of three buildings identical to this one were painted different colors. I cannot verify if these were the original colors from when the base was active, but the buildings seem untouched.

This building is the color I am used to seeing on the other remaining bases I have visited. The third building was a beige or cream color. Unfortunately, no photos can be found from when the base was active so all I can do is speculate as to whether the buildings have been altered or not. (*Photo courtesy of Charles Cormier*)

One of the two remaining radar base structures at the Caswell AFS site. The SAGE radar arrays were much larger than those used at the Nike control sites.

Security entrance, Caribou Air Force Station, aka North River Depot, aka Weapons Storage Area. This gate was a sallyport entrance which was a secure portal within a secure area. This gate is where those wishing to gain access to the weapons storage area would have had to present their credentials to gain entry. Those without credentials would be subject to immediate detainment.

Plant #2 was built in 1955 as a service and maintenance area for thermonuclear weapons. Plant #1 (which was built in 1952) was a much larger plant for the service, assembly, and maintenance of atomic weapons. Plant #1 is no longer standing and nothing remains of the structure that was once the atomic plant. During the base clean-up process, approximately 1,000 cubic yards of low-level radioactive waste from the atomic era was removed and sent to a disposal facility in Utah.[3]

The deep single bay of an atomic bomb storage igloo. The atomic storage areas were large single bay storage bunkers built to hold the extremely large fission weapons. Some thermonuclear storage igloos were built with an outer bay, or vestibule which was used as a detection area to detect radioactive gasses that may be leaking from a weapon stored within.

The weapons storage area is now under the protection of the U.S. Fish and Wildlife service and the property is maintained as a National Wildlife Refuge. For those who like to mix wildlife with Cold War artifacts, my wife and I saw a bear as we were exploring the area. So, the refuge is working well!

The nuclear storage facility contains weapons bunkers that are spread out nearly as far as the eye can see. The two igloos in the foreground were specialized tritium storage areas. At one time, there were four such storage units, but now only two remain. Tritium, coupled with lithium deuteride, were both used in conjunction with a plutonium capsule to create a thermonuclear chain reaction in hydrogen weapons.

The weapons storage area that once housed both atomic and thermonuclear weapons is very large and encompasses many acres, but there was an equally large storage area for conventional weapons as well. Despite many of the buildings and facilities being removed from the original area that was Caribou Air Force Station, many still remain, and the size of the area is still quite impressive.

Building 260 was one of the original buildings built in 1952 as a plutonium storage building. The building was designed to appear as though it were an office building to any reconnaissance conducted in the area. The second floor of the facility was solid concrete and actually a faux floor. Nuclear testing in the early 1950s determined the building would not withstand certain atomic detonations, so the upgraded design of building 272 was built in 1954. Note the high security of the building. In addition to the two concrete sentry towers, a large watchtower once used to stand behind the building.

Similar to building 260, the second floor of "A-2" building 272 was also comprised of solid concrete. Unlike building 260, building 272's storage areas were all located underground and had to be accessed via a 30-foot-long tunnel to the four storage vaults. Both buildings 260 (A building) and 272 (A-2) housed the plutonium "birdcages," and in addition the A structure held the detonator pits for atomic bombs whereas the A-2 building held booster capsules for hydrogen bombs.[4]

The Loring Alert Area with alert "Christmas Tree" or "Crow's Foot" apron. The large gate at the bottom of the picture is the gate that provided aircraft access to the main runway.

The "mole hole" was the nickname for the alert area which was built to house the alert force personnel who maintained a constant state of readiness.

Similar to the plutonium storage building (building 272), the 18,000 square-foot mole hole was a windowless concrete structure with a floor below ground. It was designed by Leo A. Daly of Omaha, NE, who designed identical structures to accommodate either seventy, 100, or 150 personnel.

Underground access to the facility is through one of several downward facing corrugated metal tubes. The windowless, underground structure was very dependent on electrical lighting and the alert area had its own power station.

Above left: A peek down inside one of the access tubes. It would have been interesting to see the mole hole when it was functional. Unfortunately, very few photos exist due to the classified nature of the facilities.

Above right: Not all the tubes are facing down. Some of them go up to the top floor. There is also roof access, giving one an opportunity to look out over the alert apron.

A surveillance tower that overlooks the entire alert area. In addition to the mole hole, alert apron, and other out-buildings, there was also a tennis court and basketball court in the alert area for off duty alert personnel to recreate.

One of the many high-security areas on the base. This entrance to the alert area had a double fenceline, a guard house with bulletproof glass, and a screening area covered with plexiglass.

A look inside the high-security gatehouse. All the outward-facing cinderblock walls have small ports in them, just large enough to fire a weapon through, and the small windows are of bulletproof glass.

The double fenceline provided a place for armed security police to patrol with their working canine sentries. With their keen senses of smell and hearing, sentry dogs were essential in the detection of enemy movement, more especially at night.

The Loring sentry dog kennel area and training yard has grown-in considerably after three decades, but this is where the dogs and their handlers worked and trained. Sentry dogs were (and still are) a vital part of security at military installations worldwide. The obedience and loyalty of canines is surpassed only by their keen senses and ferocity when called upon.

Because of the high regard that is held for the canine soldiers, they were given a place of honor at Loring.

The first-generation B-36 maintenance hangar; the star of Loring's abandoned skyline and a source of contention among some in the state of Maine.

In early 2024, the Loring Air Museum attempted to secure the arch hangar and the action had the support of local tourism interests. The Loring Development Authority squelched the attempt before it made it through legislation. The status quo of wishful thinking and waiting is the standard it seems and attempts to preserve the hangar are currently dead on the tarmac. The hangar is owned by the state of Maine, and therefore, its residents. The small board that comprises the LDA is wielding considerable power and not allowing the residents of the state to offer their opinions on the matter.

As if the arch ceiling were not enough concrete to impress, the subfoundation is reinforced concrete that is twenty inches thick which was necessary to accommodate the heavy loads of the bombers. To get a better idea of the size of this massive hangar, consider the fleet of full-sized heavy-duty trucks and the school bus that are all to the right of this picture; the size of the hangar makes them look like matchbox toys.

The control tower stands to the left, looking east toward the tarmac, down the north end of the hangar. Even now, thirty years after the jet engines have fallen silent, the base remains eerily quiet.

The blue buildings behind the tower is the location of the now defunct Maine Military Authority. There is a large solar field between the MMA and the tower, a modern addition to the base.

Looking down the taxiway south toward both the arch and DC hangars. The alert area is on the far end of the runway to the left.

Above left: The Loring AFB control tower, an iconic monument to the Cold War. Inside, the facility is equipped with a passenger terminal, weather station, and various other spaces. The facility was upgraded in 1990, and again in 1993 when a new heating system was installed. The base closed the following year. The 1996 appraisal value was $642,500.

Above right: Approach lights that are no longer lit leading to the runway at Loring. The lights helped to guide pilots to the runway as they made their final approach.

The vantage point of a pilot on final approach at Loring AFB. A runway that countless aircraft approached and took off from during the decades of the Cold War.

The double-cantilever hangar, SAC's second-generation B-36 maintenance hangar. These hangars were designed and built in three different sizes: basic, medium bomber (B-47), and heavy bomber (B-36). The latter size is what was built at Loring to hold five B-36 bombers.

When constructing the enormous foundation, a 7,000-pound hydraulic press was used to inject concrete into the ground, creating 260 concrete caissons. It was an engineering first of its kind to counteract Maine's adverse conditions. The hangar was built using more than 3,000 tons of steel and the 60-foot-tall, 30- by 35-foot doors weighed 18 to 22 tons each.

If you find the exterior of the DC hangar impressive, the interior will nearly leave you breathless. With the trussed archways and wide-open bays, the hangar offers an impressive "wow factor"! Nearly 16 miles of piping was embedded into the concrete floor for radiant heating.

Equipment in various states of disrepair left behind in the DC hangar. Also, note the three-story workshops occupying the center of the hangar. There are four of these shops in the hanger. Sixteen evenly spaced concrete encased steel columns support the roof and create corner posts for the four shops.

Looking north along the taxiway past the arch hangar and tower. Both runways are also visible to the right and extreme right of the image. In 1948, the nearly 2-mile-long taxiway was completed at a taxpayer cost of $1.8 million. The specialized bituminous concrete was used on all the airstrips.

Above left: Number 40 nose dock stands prominently along a line of nose docks. The nose docks were built in 1956 and several remain on the abandoned base.

Above right: A closer look at the doors of the nose dock. Note, the oval opening that would allow the tail of the aircraft to protrude when docked.

A view down the abandoned railroad tracks, past the DC hangar with the arch hangar in view behind it. The base had its own railroad to bring supplies and weapons into the base.

The building to the left in the photo was a fire-control water pump station, built in 1955 with a 10,000-gallon per minute capacity. The hangar in the background of the image is referred to as the snow hangar, presumably because it contained snow removal equipment.

During the initial phase of construction at Limestone in 1947, a railroad spur into the base was built connecting Limestone Airfield to the Bangor and Aroostook Railroad line in Limestone. This is a portion of the air force railroad and bridge, located outside of the base, near the town of Limestone.

The tracks crisscross the base in many areas and help contribute to the post-apocalyptic appearance of the abandoned landscape.

Not many remnants of the air force railroad remain with perhaps these three exceptions, of which only two are visible. The plow is a vintage Russell plow, and behind it is an engine shed. Not visible in the picture is the Baldwin S12 diesel-electric switcher locomotive, built in 1952 and stored in the engine shed.

The power plant for the base was part of the initial planning and construction phase and is part of the original base infrastructure.

Inside the power plant sits four massive Fairbanks-Morse generators which were used to generate power to supply the base. To help put the size of the generators into perspective, this image is the rear of the plant showing the exhaust pipes for the generators.

The solid fuel transfer and stockpile area. Right up until the base closure, a steam plant was used to heat Loring. Another use for the Loring railroad spur was the massive quantities of coal that would need to be brought in to keep the plant running. The coal would be brought here by train and dumped into a hopper then onto a conveyor. The conveyor was attached to the tower in the image, which in turn has conveyors protruding from each side that would send the coal out onto the large concrete area.

Above left: Other concerns in the nearby tank-farm are that jet fuel may have leaked into the ground. The area that was once Loring AFB is a government SUPERFUND cleanup site and many mitigations have been performed. Environmental investigations and testing are still ongoing.

Above right: It is uncertain how long these two behemoths have been lumbering in the woods. The Loring pipeline was put into use seventy-one years ago and these tanks are at the termination point of the pipeline, in the petroleum, oil, and lubrication (POL) area.

According to EPA reports, Loring had three on-site landfills when it closed. All three were capped, but not before two of them had contaminated soil, sediments, and sludge added to them during the base cleanup and mitigation process.[5]

There are four jet fuel tanks still at Loring and this is the fourth and final tank I feature in this book. It is located at the fuel transfer station near the flight line. According to a 1996 inventory and appraisal report, this pump station was built in 1954.

The base laundry and dry-cleaning facility was built in 1957 and had a new roof installed with other upgrades in 1990–1991; the building's 1996 appraisal was $110,000. In the area surrounding the building, there are many groundwater test sites due to recent discoveries of Per- and polyfluoroalkyl substances (PFAS). An ongoing investigation began by the air force in 2015.[6]

The base movie theater was built in 1955 and has a 1,000-seat capacity. New seats and a stage were added in 1988. There was no appraisal listed due to its limited use potential.

The base library was built in 1958 and its fair market value in 1996 was listed at $240,000.

During its use, this was a survival-equipment shop and the brown tower to the rear of the building is a parachute drying tower. The facility was built in 1956 and its 1996 appraisal was $35,000.

This 1953 dental clinic was listed in the 1996 inventory as having an asbestos shingled roof. Nothing else is stated about it other than its valuation of $26,250.

This structure was the religious education center and chapel, built in 1957 and completely renovated between 1986–1988.

The former wing command headquarters and administrative complex was built in 1952. Extensive renovations were done to the complex from 1987–1991 and a new heating system was installed in 1995, a year after the base closure.

This abandoned military housing complex is very surreal to visit. Parents no longer rush off to avoid being late and children no longer wait for the school bus. The entire neighborhood is silent and barren.

A drone image of a section of identical abandoned structures that were once homes in one of the base housing areas.

It is not just the base that has been left behind. This mobile home park just outside of Loring does not look like it survived the Cold War, but rather, it ironically resembles a post-apocalyptic landscape that is often associated with a nuclear attack.

13

CONCLUSION

It is true that we cannot evolve and grow if we continually look to the past, and we cannot expand if we hold onto everything that we have ever built, but Loring AFB represents an extremely volatile period in human history when two nation's mutually assured annihilation was the only thing preventing a nuclear holocaust. The monumental expenditures, top secret weapons movements, and the transformation of small-town rural Maine into a national defense stronghold and strategic nuclear weapons operational stockpile might be something to consider preserving.

On April 8, 2024, the United States witnessed a solar eclipse and the region of Loring AFB (now known as the Loring Commerce Center) experienced totality during the event. Law enforcement officials estimate that more than 20,000 people traveled to Aroostook County for the eclipse and the Loring Development Authority hosted a viewing event at the arch hangar, bringing the area more visitors than it has seen in one day in over a decade. The rock band Phish played on the flightline on three separate occasions and each time well over 50,000 people came to the area, briefly making Limestone one of the most populated towns in Maine in 1997, 1998, and 2003.

It begs the notion that perhaps it could be made a Cold War destination of sorts. In other parts of the country, Cold War relics have been made into state parks, private attractions, and federally preserved spaces. They all boast considerable tourist traffic. Currently, the United States Fish and Wildlife Service has control of most of the former Caribou Air Station, and it has been made into a National Wildlife Refuge, so the former weapons storage area is now largely preserved. Perhaps it is time for the people of Maine to consider the possibility of assisting Aroostook County in turning the hangars, flightline, and alert area, all of them or select portions, into a Cold War recreational park to preserve the area's incredible history, draw tourism into the area, and help create local jobs and revenue.

ENDNOTES

Chapter 1

1 Orwell, George, "You and the Atom Bomb," *Tribune*, October 19, 1945.
2 Churchill, Winston, 1874–1965, The Sinews of Peace, Post-War Speeches (Boston: Houghton Mifflin Co., 1949).
3 National Archives and Records Administration, Office of Presidential Libraries, Harry S. Truman Library, "Churchill, Truman, and Stalin at Potsdam," National Archives, July 23, 1945, catalog.archives.gov/id/348307517. Accessed June 6, 2024.
4 National Archives and Records Administration, Office of Presidential Libraries, Harry S. Truman Library, "Nagasaki, Japan, Under Atomic Bomb Attack," National Archives, August 9, 1945, catalog.archives.gov/id/204836584. Accessed June 6, 2024.
5 Rowe, Abbie, and NPS, "Truman and Churchill at End of Train," National Archives, March 4, 1946, catalog.archives.gov/id/338955488. Accessed June 6, 2024.

Chapter 2

1 Delano, Jack, "Potato Fields Just outside Caribou, Maine, along the Banks of the Aroostook River," Library of Congress, www.loc.gov/pictures/item/2017792474/. Accessed June 6, 2024.
2 "Bangor and Aroostook Railroad Station, Limestone, Maine," National Archives, date unknown, catalog.archives.gov/id/44171656. Accessed June 6, 2024.

Chapter 3

1 "Two Bases for the Biggest Strategic Bombers," *Engineering News-Record*, February 28, 1957, p. 40.
2 Farthing, Jonathan D., "Completion and Mission of Loring AFB," *Historic Building Inventory and Evaluation Loring Air Force Base, Maine* (Department of Defense, Brooks AFB, TX, 1998), 3.38.
3 Farthing, Jonathan D., "3.4.3 Completion and Mission of Loring AFB," *Historic Building Inventory and Evaluation Loring Air Force Base, Maine* (Department of Defense, Brooks AFB, TX, 1998), 3.42.
4 U.S. Army Air Forces, Washington D.C., "AAF's Newest Superbomber, the XB-36, Compared with Veteran B-29," Library of Congress, *c.* 1942, www.loc.gov/pictures/item/89713621/. Accessed June 6, 2024.

5 Farthing, Jonathan D., "Completion and Mission of Loring AFB," *Historic Building Inventory and Evaluation Loring Air Force Base, Maine* (Department of Defense, Brooks AFB, TX, 1998), 4.33.
6 "Loring AFB Arch Hanger 1948." *Get Archive*, marcoswentworth1.getarchive.net/media/loring-afb-arch-hanger-1948-e30116. Accessed June 5, 2024.
7 "B-36 USAF," *American Aviation Historical Society*, date unknown, aahs.getarchive.net/media/b-36-usafm-install-1. Accessed June 5, 2024.
8 Parkman, Aubrey, *Army Engineers in New England: The Military and Civil Work of the Corps of Engineers in New England, 1775–1975* (U.S. Army Corps of Engineers, 1978), p. 147.
9 War Department, Office of the Chief of Engineers, Boston District, "Parking Apron, Aerial View, Limestone Air Force Base, Limestone, Maine," National Archives, *c.* 1956, catalog.archives.gov/id/44171660. Accessed June 6, 2024.
10 War Department, Office of the Chief of Engineers, Boston District, "Nose Hangar, Limestone Air Force Base, Limestone, Maine," National Archives, date unknown, catalog.archives.gov/id/44171658. Accessed June 6, 2024.
11 Loring Air Museum, "DC Hangar," Loring Air Museum, date unknown, loringairmuseum.com/photo-galleries. Full use is granted by the Loring Air Museum.
12 War Department, Office of the Chief of Engineers, Boston District, "Loring Runway Center," National Archives, November 1, 1961, catalog.archives.gov/id/24902501. Accessed June 6, 2024.
13 War Department, Office of the Chief of Engineers, Boston District, "Noncommissioned Officers Club Housing, Limestone Air Force Base, Limestone, Maine," National Archives, date unknown, catalog.archives.gov/id/44171662. Accessed June 6, 2024.
14 "Oblique Aerial Photograph of Flightline Showing Building 8280 (Double Cantilever Hangar)," Library of Congress, January 18, 1968, www.loc.gov/pictures/item/me0308.photos.319700p/. Accessed June 6, 2024.
15 Bates, Jeff, "Interior View Looking Northeast, Showing Three Story Concrete Shop Structures Dividing Hangar into Three Work Bays," Library of Congress, 1968, www.loc.gov/item/me0310/. Accessed June 6, 2024.
16 Department of Defense, "Front View of a KC-135R Stratotanker," National Archives, October 1, 1993, catalog.archives.gov/id/6494688. Accessed June 6, 2024.
17 Pollanen, SSGT Russ, "A View of the Sign at the Base's Main Gate," National Archives, October 1, 1989, catalog.archives.gov/id/644901388. Accessed June 6, 2024.

Chapter 4

1 Kelly, Lt. Gen. Joe W., "If Deterrence Fails," *White Falcon*, Volume X, Number 35 (Headquarters, Air Forces Iceland), October 8, 1960, p. 2.
2 Garbinski, John C., *The United States Air Force in Maine* (Maine Aviation Historical Society, 1998), p. 75.
3 Pollanen, SSGT Russ, "Oblique Aerial Photograph Showing Weapons Storage Area, from Master Plan of Caribou AFS," Library of Congress, date unknown, hdl.loc.gov/loc.pnp/hhh.me0311/photos.319786p. Accessed June 6, 2024.
4 Loring Air Museum, "Command/Control Building. Q Area, Caribou AFS," Loring Air Museum, date unknown, loringairmuseum.com/photo-galleries. Full use is granted by the Loring Air Museum.
5 Vanden Brink, Brian, "Interior, Building 272 (Plutonium Storage Building)," Library of Congress, 1999, hdl.loc.gov/loc.pnp/hhh.me0311/photos.319788p. Accessed June 6, 2024.
6 Vanden Brink, Brian, "Interior, Building 272 (Plutonium Storage Building)," Library of Congress, 1999, hdl.loc.gov/loc.pnp/hhh.me0311/photos.319790p. Accessed June 6, 2024.
7 "42d Air Wing Defense B-36," Archives.Gov, Public Domain, via Wikimedia Commons, date unknown, commons.wikimedia.org/wiki/File:42d_Air_Wing_Defense_b-36.jpg. Accessed June 6, 2024.

Chapter 5

1 Weitze, Ph.D., Karen J., *Cold War Infrastructure for Strategic Air Command: The Bomber Mission* (United States Army Corps of Engineers, 1999), p. 108.
2 Weitze, Ph.D., Karen J., *Cold War Infrastructure for Strategic Air Command: The Bomber Mission* (United States Army Corps of Engineers, 1999), p. 120.
3 "B-47 Stratojet," U.S. Department of Defense, date unknown, media.defense.gov/2004/Jan/20/2000595213/-1/-1/0/020903-O-9999R-001.JPG. Accessed June 6, 2024.

Chapter 6

1 "Decision to Drop the Atomic Bomb," National Archives, Harry S. Truman Library, date unknown, www.trumanlibrary.gov/sites/default/files/atomic-bomb.jpg. Accessed June 6, 2024.
2 Wikipedia contributors, "1958 Tybee Island mid-air collision," Wikipedia, The Free Encyclopedia, May 25, 2024. Web. June 20, 2024.
3 "MK 15 Nuclear Bomb," Wikipedia, date unknown, en.wikipedia.org/wiki/1958_Tybee_Island_mid-air_collision#/media/File:Mk15.jpg. Accessed June 6, 2024.
4 "A Hound Dog Guided Missile Passes in Review at the Inaugural Parade for JFK," National Archives, January 20, 1961, catalog.archives.gov/id/218517938. Accessed June 6, 2024.
5 "Airmen from the 42nd Munitions Maintenance Squadron Prepare to Load a Mark 60 CAPTOR," National Archives, November 1, 1989, catalog.archives.gov/id/6449017. Accessed June 6, 2024.

Chapter 7

1 Moeller, Col. Stephen P., "Vigilant and Invincible," *ADA (Air Defense Artillery) Magazine*, May–June 1995, p. 9.
2 Moeller, Col. Stephen P., "Vigilant and Invincible," *ADA (Air Defense Artillery) Magazine*, May–June 1995, p. 16.
3 Wolf, Richard I., *Air Staff Historical Study*, 1987, p. 219. Collins-Vand Agreement.
4 The Flint Journal #415012, 1955, image.mlive.com/home/mlive-media/pgfull/img/flint-journal/photo/2014/11/20/-3b1a71be68038bfa.jpg. Accessed June 6, 2024.
5 "Aerial View of Nike Missile Site PH 07L," National Archives, October 20, 1959, catalog.archives.gov/id/266694368. Accessed June 6, 2024.
6 "Unidentified Launch Area with Personnel Door, Decontamination Shower and Ajax Missiles," Library of Congress, date unknown, hdl.loc.gov/loc.pnp/hhh.ri0411/photos.363276p. Accessed June 6, 2024.
7 "Project 26 - Operation Dominic," National Archives, 1946–1962, catalog.archives.gov/id/146764280. Accessed June 6, 2024.

Chapter 8

1 "Civil Defense Staff College," National Archives, 1951–1961, catalog.archives.gov/id/7385136. Accessed June 6, 2024.
2 Freeman, ED., E.C. "Sage: Semi-Automatic Ground Environment Air Defense System," *MIT Lincoln Laboratory*, www.ll.mit.edu/about/history/sage-semi-automatic-ground-environment-air-defense-system. Accessed May 24, 2024.

Chapter 10

1 Werrell, Kenneth P., *The Evolution of the Cruise Missile* (Air University Press, 1985), p. 92.
2 Garbinski, John C., *The United States Air Force in Maine* (Maine Aviation Historical Society, 1998), p. 50.

Chapter 11

1 "AGM-28 Hound Dog," *Wikipedia*, Wikimedia Foundation, April 26, 2024, en.wikipedia.org/wiki/AGM-28_Hound_Dog. Accessed June 10, 2024.
2 *Cold War: Soldiers of God*, directed by Kenneth Branagh, Warner Brothers, 2012.
3 Kraft, Victor, *The History of Loring Air Force Base* (Bessey and Kraft, 2000), p. 133.
4 Robinson, Peter, "Tear Down This Wall," *Prologue Magazine*, vol. 39, no. 2, 2007, doi.org/https://www.archives.gov/publications/prologue/2007/summer/berlin.html. Accessed June 4, 2024.
5 "Civil Engineering Crews Use Snow Removal Equipment to Clear a Ramp," National Archives, January 1, 1995, catalog.archives.gov/id/6389031. Accessed June 1, 2024.
6 Belcher, TSGT Boyd, "AGM-69 Short Range Attack Missiles (SRAMS) and Mark 28 Thermo-nuclear Bombs," National Archives, April 1, 1984, catalog.archives.gov/id/6388711. Accessed June 1, 2024.
7 "President Ronald Reagan during His Visit to Checkpoint Charlie," National Archives, June 11, 1982, catalog.archives.gov/id/75856859. Accessed June 1, 2024.
8 "President Ronald Reagan and Soviet General Secretary Gorbachev Signing The Inf Treaty in The East Room," National Archives, December 8, 1987, catalog.archives.gov/id/75855867. Accessed June 1, 2024.

Chapter 12

1 Valigra, Lori, "Aroostook Centre Mall Sells for $4.65 Million," *TheCounty*, March 11, 2019, thecounty.me/2019/03/11/news/aroostook-centre-mall-sells-for-4-65-million/.
2 Farthing, Jonathan D., "Completion and Mission of Loring AFB," *Historic Building Inventory and Evaluation Loring Air Force Base, Maine* (Department of Defense, Brooks AFB, TX, 1998), 4.1.
3 "Superfund Site: Loring Air Force Base Limestone, ME," *United States Environmental Protection Agency*, cumulis.epa.gov/supercpad/cursites/csitinfo.cfm?id=0101074. Accessed May 28, 2024.
4 Weitze, Ph.D., Karen J., *Cold War Infrastructure for Strategic Air Command: The Bomber Mission* (United States Army Corps of Engineers, 1999), p. 100.
5 "Superfund Site: Loring Air Force Base Limestone, ME," *United States Environmental Protection Agency*, cumulis.epa.gov/supercpad/SiteProfiles/index.cfm?fuseactionid=0101074. Accessed May 28, 2024.
6 Lizotte, Melissa, "PFAS Found on Former Loring Base Could Delay $4B Fuel Production Project," *The County*, December 22, 2023, PFAS found on former Loring base could delay $4B fuel production project. Accessed May 26, 2024.

FURTHER READING

On North River Depot: Garbinski, John C., *North River Depot* (Lulu, 2021)
On Loring AFB: Johndro, Cuppy, *Loring A.F.B., A comprehensive History* (Lulu, 2024)